With a passion for cooking, River, a 4-year-old blossoming chef, dives into a step-by-step simple recipe book with imagination & flare. River shows her dazzling cooking style as she dives into 3 meals... Princess' Breakfast, Superhero Lunch & Fairy's Desert.

Sweet River's Recipes
Shaneka & River Demps

That's me.... I'm River!

Princesses like to cook breakfast... you know?
Super Hero's are great lunch chefs... you see?
Fairies love to bake treats that glow!
Follow me... I will show you the best recipes!
Love,
River.

River

Mommy says that you must always start off your day with a good breakfast.
What should we make? I know...

Princess' Breakfast:
Sparkly Hot cocoa with whipped cream, marshmallows, and glitter
What we need: Milk, Chocolate syrup, whipped cream, edible glitter (any color)

Step: 1. Pour chocolate syrup. Into Milk
Step: 2. Stir until it's brown just like you like it.
Step: 3. Swirl whip cream over the top.
Step: 4. Sprinkle marshmallows and glitter.

Princess' Scrambled Eggs with shredded cheese and bacon

What we need: Eggs, shredded cheese, bacon pieces, butter

Step: 1. Crack 2 eggs in a bowl. *Make sure that we look for any shells.

Step: 2. Sprinkle in 3 pinches of cheese and stir.

Step: 3. Pour into pan of butter (mommy will need to help us with this part for sure).

Step: 4. Turn the eggs in the pan (mommy will tell us when they are ready and put them on the plate).

Step: 5. Sprinkle 1 pinch of cheese and 2 pinches of bacon on top.

1
2
3
4
5

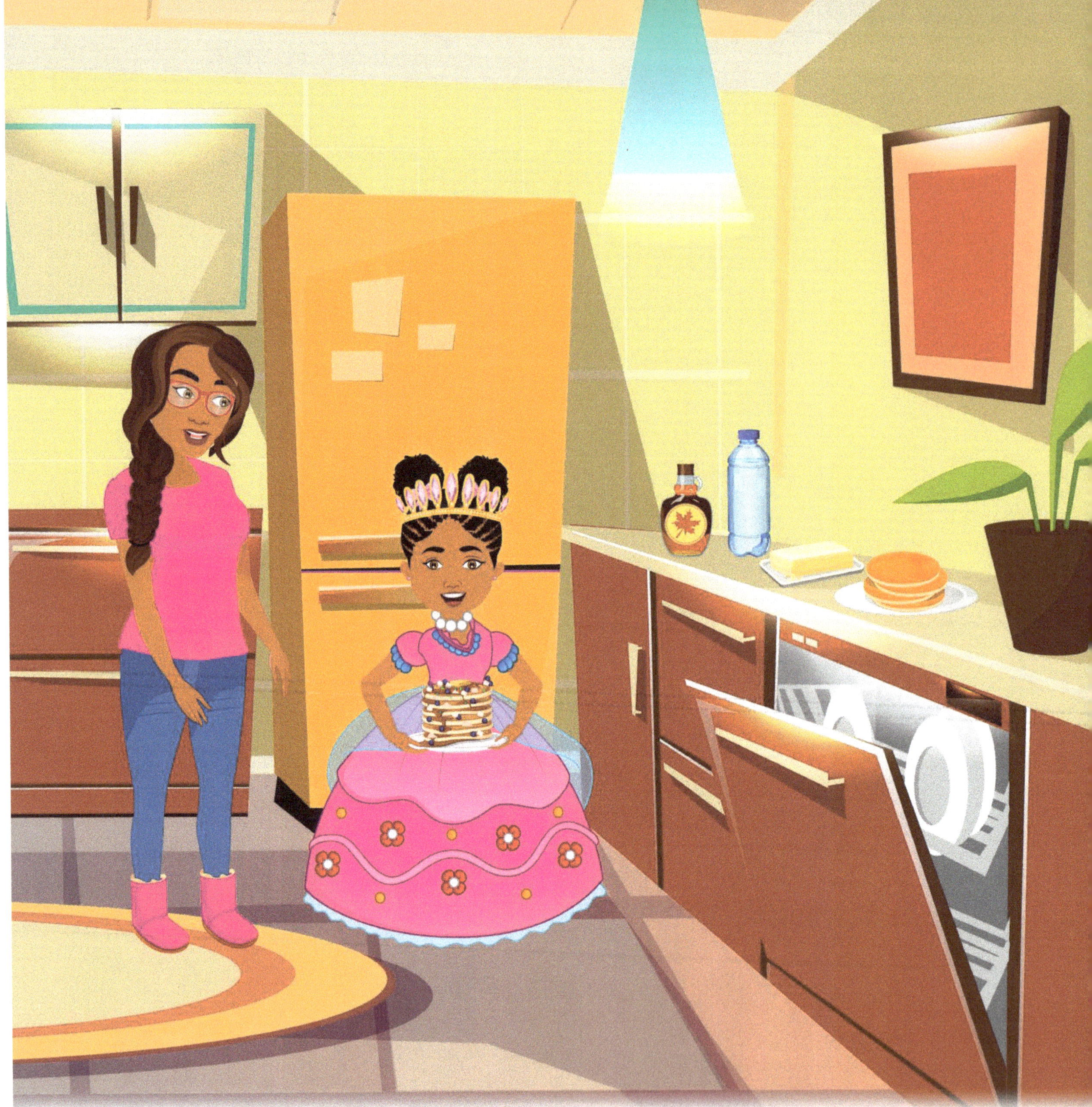

What we need: Lucky Charms pancake mix, water, butter, syrup

Step: 1. Stir Pancake Mix and water in a bowl. It will be lumpy a little but that is okay.

Step: 2. Cook until golden brown on both sides (this is mommy's part).

Step: 3. On a plate, put 1 small spoon of butter on top.

Step: 4. Drizzle syrup and cereal topping on top.

Super Hero's Lunch/Dinner:
Yummy Hero Cakes

What we need: Biscuits, ground beef (cooked) mixed with taco seasoning and ¼ cup water (mommy's part), shredded cheese, sour cream, non-stick spray

Step: 1. Spray cupcake pan with nonstick spray.

Step: 2. Open biscuits and put into cupcake pan.

Step: 3. Put 2 spoons of beef mix on to each biscuit.

Step: 4. Sprinkle 2 finger pinches of shredded cheese on to each biscuit.

Step: 5. Mommy will bake our biscuits in the oven and let us know when they are done and cooled off.

Step: 6. Drop 1 spoon of sour cream on your biscuit and yummmmmyyyy.

♡1♡
♡2♡
♡3♡
♡4♡
♡5♡
♡6♡

Flying Pepperoni and Sausage Pizza

What we need: Pizza Crust (dry), pizza sauce, shredded mozzarella cheese, olive oil, pepperoni, crumbled sausage (cooked)

Step: 1. Place pizza crust on pizza stone or pan.

Step: 2. Use a spoon to put sauce all over the crust, but not too much.

Step: 3. Sprinkle cheese all over pizza. The more the better.

Step: 4. Place pepperoni and sausage all over, just like you like it.

Step: 5. Paint the edges with a brush of olive oil.

Step: 6. Mommy will bake our pizza just right and let us know when its all cooled to eat.

Fairy Deserts:

Fairy Cupcakes with icing, sprinkles or glitter

What we need - Cake: 1 box of Confetti Cake Mix, 3 eggs, 1 cup water, 1/3 cup Oil

Step: 1. Mommy will preheat the oven to 350 degrees.

Step: 2. In a big bowl, pour the cake mix, water, oil and eggs.

Step: 3. Blend with a hand mixer for 2 minutes- medium. Mommy will help us with this part.

Step: 4. Pour our cake batter into a baking dish and into the oven to bake (with mommy's help... she will let us know when its all baked and cooled).

Fairy Cupcakes with icing, sprinkles or glitter

What we need – Icing: 2 cups-Powdered sugar, ½ cup-butter, 2 tablespoons-milk, 3 drops-vanilla extract, 3 drops-food coloring, edible glitter

      Step: 1. Put butter into a bowl.

      Step: 2. Mix with mommy's help until smooth.

      Step: 3. Add in sugar and mix in.

      Step: 4. Add in milk and mix for 3-4 minutes.

      Step: 5. Add in food coloring until it looks just like we like.

      Step: 6. Decorate our cupcakes with icing, glitter or sprinkles or other yummies.

Cooking is so fun, I knew that we could....
Baking sparkly, super yummy food, I knew that we would!
Princesses, Super Hero's, Fairies.... Go Figure...
We can all do it,
with Love....
River

The End

Now it's *time* to
Create your own recipes

You Can Do it!

Create your own recipes

Items you will need:

Step 1-

Step 2-

Step 3-

Step 4-

Step 5-

Pictures:

Create your own recipes

Items you will need:

Step 1-

Step 2-

Step 3-

Step 4-

Step 5-

Pictures:

Create your own recipes

Items you will need:

Step 1-

Step 2-

Step 3-

Step 4-

Step 5-

Pictures:

Create your own recipes

Items you will need:

Step 1-

Step 2-

Step 3-

Step 4-

Step 5-

Pictures:

River, River
Ocean Blue…
River, River
Mommy Loves
YOU!

Thank you

Grandma Lillian & Veronica, Mommy & Daddy, and Siblings (Reggie, Dashelle, Nick, Nana, & Nate), for showing me that I **can do** anything!
Illustration by:Alqadir_786

Written by: Shaneka & River Demps